VIDEO
SHARING

GLOBAL CITIZENS: SOCIAL MEDIA

Published in the United States of America by Cherry Lake Publishing
Ann Arbor, Michigan
www.cherrylakepublishing.com

Content Adviser: Marcus Collins, MBA, Chief Consumer Connections Officer, Marketing Professor
Reading Adviser: Marla Conn MS, Ed., Literacy specialist, Read-Ability, Inc.

Library of Congress Cataloging-in-Publication Data

Names: Orr, Tamra, author.
Title: Video sharing / Tamra B. Orr.
Description: Ann Arbor : Cherry Lake Publishing, [2019] | Series: Global citizens: social media |
    Audience: Grade 4 to 6. | Includes bibliographical references and index.
Identifiers: LCCN 2018035591 | ISBN 9781534143098 (hardcover) | ISBN 9781534139657 (pbk.) |
    ISBN 9781534140851 (pdf) | ISBN 9781534142053 (hosted ebook)
Subjects: LCSH: Digital video—Social aspects—Juvenile literature. | Social media—Juvenile literature.
Classification: LCC TK6680.5 .O77 2019 | DDC 302.23/1—dc23
LC record available at https://lccn.loc.gov/2018035591

Cherry Lake Publishing would like to acknowledge the work of the Partnership for 21st Century Learning.
Please visit www.p21.org for more information.

Printed in the United States of America
Corporate Graphics

ABOUT THE AUTHOR

Tamra Orr is the author of more than 500 nonfiction books for readers of all ages. A graduate of Ball State University, she now lives in the Pacific Northwest with her family. When she isn't writing books, she is either camping, reading, or on the computer researching the latest topic.

TABLE OF CONTENTS

CHAPTER 1

History: Lights, Camera, Action!

Want to make a pizza but don't know how?

Need pointers on how to land that kickflip on your skateboard?

Hope to learn Spanish by the end of the summer?

Desperate for help on that algebra problem you're stuck on?

All this information is right at our fingertips. It's available on videos that others have created and posted to a **web hosting service**. Video sharing, as it's termed, is the fastest growing activity on the internet. Millions of videos are uploaded to the internet every day in staggering numbers—from those shot in someone's backyard with a phone to professional-quality footage filmed with high-tech cameras.

Jawed Karim (not pictured), Chad Hurley, and Steven Chen used to work at PayPal when it was still a start-up.

A Trip to the Zoo

Jawed Karim, Chad Hurley, and Steven Chen had come up with a new idea. Over dinner one night in December of 2004, the three friends talked about starting a new website featuring videos on a large variety of topics. "Video, we felt, really wasn't being addressed on the Internet," stated Hurley. "People were collecting video clips on their cell phones . . . but there was no easy way to share." That was the night the idea for YouTube was born. But it wasn't until Jawed Karim went to the San Diego Zoo in April 2005 and uploaded a 19-second video about elephants' trunks that the internet was officially revolutionized.

YouTube hit 1 billion views in just 4 years after launching!

YouTube Makes Its Mark

Since it was launched in February 2005, YouTube has done nothing but grow. Seven months after launching, one of YouTube's videos, a Nike ad, hit 1 million views! A year later, Google bought YouTube for $1.65 billion. YouTube has hit a number of milestones since then, including allowing users to earn money from their videos, partnering with CNN to cover breaking news, offering movie rentals, adding banner ads, and featuring concerts and other events live. In 2012, a wacky South Korean music video helped YouTube reach 1 billion views on a single video!

While there are other types of video sharing sites on the internet today, there is no doubt that YouTube is the biggest. As the third most frequently visited website on the internet, it offers viewers virtually countless hours of videos to teach, entertain, appall, scare, amuse, and educate.

YouTube Timeline

February 2005	YouTube website purchased
April 2005	First video released—*Me at the Zoo*
September 2005	First video to hit 1 million views—Nike's *Touch of Gold*
October 2006	Purchased by Google for $1.65 billion
May 2007	Allowed users to get paid for **viral** content
May 2007	First video to go viral—*Charlie Bit My Finger*
August 2007	First advertising banners appeared
April 2011	Featured live events
April 2017	YouTube TV launched

Videos on social media platforms are shared over 1,200 percent more than text or image posts combined!

Instagram Takes Over

YouTube isn't the only go-to place for entertaining and educational videos. In 2011, Snapchat launched—taking the social media and video sharing world by storm. Snapchat is a video-sharing messaging app that allows users to "share moments" and short 10-second "stories." Not one to be overshadowed, Instagram stepped in next. It had begun as a photo-sharing service in 2010, but in 2013 launched 15-second video clips. Three years later, the company added Instagram Stories, similar to Snapchat Stories, and lengthened the 15-second clips to 60 seconds—further taking the lead from Snapchat. Instagram also launched its IGTV feature in June 2018. The feature allows users to post videos up to 1 hour long. Some people believe Instagram hopes to one day take the lead from YouTube as the number one video sharing platform with this new rollout.

Developing Questions

*How do you best learn new information? There are different types of learners, but the main types are visual, **kinesthetic**, and **auditory**. Visual learners learn best when they can see and read the information, like in a textbook. Kinesthetic, or hands-on, learners learn best when they're moving around. Auditory learners learn best when they can hear the information, like in a classroom or **podcast**. People can also be a combination of all three. This is where online videos can be incredibly helpful. They give people the chance to learn by seeing, doing, and hearing. If people want to know how to fry an egg, replace a fuse, or update a computer, they can turn to the countless online videos that show them, step-by-step, how to do so. What kind of learner do you think you are? How does watching videos help you— or not help you—when it is time to learn something new?*

CHAPTER 2

Geography: Hard to Control

When you think about viewing videos, which country do you imagine views the most? Many people would guess the United States or Canada, but they would be wrong.

The Middle East

According to an early 2018 study, the top two countries that spend the most time viewing online videos are Saudi Arabia and Turkey. In these two countries, 95 percent of internet users watch online videos. Another study puts the Middle East and North Africa in second place for the number of YouTube videos, 300 million of them, viewed every day! In fact, watching online videos in three Middle Eastern countries—the United Arab Emirates, Saudi Arabia, and Turkey—exceeded the global average

There are several countries that have censored or completely banned YouTube, including North Korea, Iran, Pakistan, China, Thailand, Libya, Turkey, Brazil, and Russia.

in 2016. About 70 percent of smartphone users in these three countries watched videos on social media at least once a week, versus the 65 percent of people globally. Studies indicate that this might be because the use of social media apps on smartphones in these countries had drastically increased that year.

Why do the people in Saudi Arabia spend so much time online viewing videos? More than half of the population is under the age of 35. They are young, curious, and eager to socialize, but they reside in countries that often **censor** what is on television or in

YouTube is available in 76 languages and 88 countries.

According to a study, 42 percent of Snapchat users in Saudi Arabia use the social media platform as soon as they wake up!

the media. Men and women who are not related are not allowed to mingle in public areas. This can be very frustrating for people. While social networking sites like Facebook and Twitter are government controlled, YouTube, Snapchat, and Instagram are not (for now). Some claim it's because these platforms are growing too fast for the government to oversee every video post. This means that video sharing offers people in countries like Saudi Arabia a freedom of expression and thought found nowhere else. Entertainment and music videos are the most popular choices, followed closely by sports.

As of May 2018, there were 80 million Snapchatters in North America and 60 million in Europe!

South Africa

Although YouTube and other video sharing sites are far more limited in South Africa, the number of users continues to grow. Of the 55.2 million people in South Africa in 2017, about 15 million were on social media, with YouTube being the second most used social platform. Currently, the most popular YouTube channels are Caspar (comedy), Kruger Sightings (animals), and MCPEMike (how to build things in *Minecraft*).

Gathering and Evaluating Sources

Have you ever watched a video with terrible sound, bad lighting, or an inferior camera? The information in the video might be great or funny or helpful, but it is irrelevant if other factors interfere. Spend some time online looking at a variety of videos, and pay close attention to the sound quality, the lighting, and other aspects. What can you learn from the videos that are excellent—and the ones that are not? What lessons can you learn about producing a high-quality video from these examples? Evaluate this information to see what you can apply to any future videos you might want to make.

CHAPTER 3

Civics: Keeping Current, Getting Involved

It may be hard to imagine, but video sharing has transformed the world in many significant ways. While videos about cute cats, eye shadow techniques, and gaming tips may not have a great deal of impact, other videos do. Videos have given many people the chance to speak out, to share an idea with the world, to promote a mission or philosophy, and to bring attention to a serious problem. This is especially true when a video goes viral—reaching thousands, or even millions, of people.

Many charitable organizations like Charity: Water, use social video platforms, like Instagram's IGTV, to engage with its viewers.

Viral Videos in the Middle East and North Africa

Between 2009 and 2011, countless videos were posted from the Middle East, highlighting a period of protests known as "Arab Spring" and "Arab Awakening." Many of these videos were **graphic** and violent. But they were honest. Jeffrey Ghannam, a journalist who covered the protests, said, "The Internet has provided an immeasurable opportunity for people in the Middle East and

Developing Claims and Using Evidence

Video sharing has grown so fast that it is almost impossible to grasp some of the numbers around it. Recent statistics say that approximately 5 billion videos are viewed every day and that 300 hours of video are uploaded to the internet every minute. There is more video content uploaded to the internet in a single month than all of the major U.S. television networks have created in 30 years! Research how video sharing might be disrupting TV networks. Do you think video sharing platforms like YouTube, Snapchat, and Instagram Stories will take over television shows or movies? Why or why not? Research this topic further using your local library and the internet. Use the information you find to support your claim.

About 28 percent of charitable organizations have a channel on YouTube.

North Africa to tell their stories through their own voices and with their own eyes." These videos played an important role in creating change in these countries. Brutal leaders found themselves exposed to the entire world for their cruel actions. Internationally, people objected, governments got involved, and change was made.

Back at Home

Video sharing is an important part of American politics and government, too. In July 2007, YouTube teamed up with news channel CNN to host the presidential debates. Citizens around

According to a study, charitable messages on YouTube had more than double the engagement from viewers compared to videos without a charitable message.

the country could watch and submit questions to be asked. Less than 2 years later, Congress launched its own official channels on YouTube so the public would have access to their representatives. By 2012, the speeches from the Democratic National Convention and the Republican National Convention were being live-streamed.

Today, YouTube and other video sharing sites are considered one of the best sources for up-to-date news, government announcements, and political **campaigning**. Anyone—from people on the scene of a disaster to people witnessing important world events to protesters—can film, upload, and share an event with the entire world in minutes. And they can even do it as it's happening! These unfiltered, up-close videos of world events are helping people of all ages keep current, become aware, and get involved.

CHAPTER 4

Economics: Vloggers and Ads

When you visit your favorite video sharing platform, what do you see? Chances are you'll probably spot a few different types of ads. The ad might be a banner across the top page or off to the side. It could be in the form of a brief commercial before a clip you want to watch. On Instagram, it could be a short clip between your friends' stories. These ads might be a little annoying—but they are a huge way for **retailers** and companies to make money. And it's not just companies that make money. **Vloggers** with a large enough following can, too.

Snapchat makes money from various types of ads, like sponsored geofilters and lenses, Snapchat Discover ads, and even ads that unlock a special feature after a user "snaps" it!

It Pays to Vlog

YouTube vloggers are making a big enough splash to create new directions for themselves. They've snagged book deals and roles in TV shows, full-length movies, and documentaries.

Top Video Sharing Sites

Site	Specializing In
YouTube	Absolutely everything
Vimeo	Movies and television shows
Metacafe	Short videos with a focus on simplicity and trending issues
Periscope	App owned by Twitter that allows users to share and stream live video
DropShots	Family-oriented materials, often used for sharing videos and pictures with family and friends

The category that receives the highest number of video uploads (41 percent) on YouTube is "People & Blogs."

Some YouTubers have made millions. In 2017, the top two highest-paid YouTubers were 26-year-old Daniel Middleton (DanTDM) and 25-year-old Evan Fong (VanossGaming). Middleton made $16.5 million for his daily reviews and **gameplay** videos of *Minecraft*. He's even married to another *Minecraft* YouTube star—Jemma Middleton, or as YouTube knows her, JemPlaysMC. Fong made about $15.5 million and is also known for posting comedic montage videos of him playing different video games.

And then there is Ryan of Ryan ToysReview. In 2015, when he was just 4 years old, he became a multimillionaire before he even started kindergarten! It was all thanks to a video of him opening and reviewing a box of toys that went viral. In 2017, he made $11 million and was on *Forbes'* list of highest-paid YouTubers. Currently, his YouTube channel has more subscribers than Disney's.

Communicating Conclusions

Before you read this book, did you watch videos online? What are your favorite types of videos to watch on YouTube or Instagram Stories? Are a few of your favorites how-to videos? How-to videos are actually the most popular videos streamed (after music videos). Share your favorite videos with your friends and family. Discuss what your goals were when you watched them. Did you want to be entertained or learn something? Discuss how often and how long you watch videos for. Do you sometimes find yourself easily distracted—watching one video right after another?

IGTV, Instagram's long-form video service, is currently ad-free to attract viewers and creators.

According to a survey, 90 percent of people confirm that videos about a product or service are helpful in their decision process.

Millions of Views ≠ Millions of Dollars

Figuring out how much money a vlogger's video has made varies from clip to clip. It depends on a number of things—from the ads played before the video to the banner ads placed on the video itself to where the viewers are located to what time of year people watch. According to a YouTube executive, a YouTube video, on average, can make a vlogger or content creator about $3 for every 1,000 views. But according to many studies, most vloggers and content creators on the platform are earning as little as $0.0006 per view. This means that a vlogger's video that had 1 million views would potentially only make $600!

Vloggers

Recently, YouTube has made it a little harder for vloggers to make money. Before, vloggers could start making money off their videos after attracting more than 10,000 total views on their videos. But after a few scandals in 2017 concerning hate speech, racial slurs, and inappropriate content that had made its way up the platform, many big brands like Pepsi and Walmart pulled their ads from YouTube. They were concerned that their ads would be associated with inappropriate content. Because of this, YouTube now requires vloggers to have at least 4,000 hours of total views within a 12-month period and more than 1,000 subscribers.

Taking Informed Action

Have you ever watched or shared a video about a charity or **nonprofit**? A recent study demonstrated that people who take the time to publicly share a video on social media are also more willing to volunteer for those same organizations. Next time you are online, check out a few of these types of videos and give some thought to sharing them with your friends and family. You might just inspire someone (even yourself!) to get involved.

Think About It

In 2016, almost three-quarters (73 percent) of all internet traffic was spent watching videos. The majority was on sites like YouTube. According to a 2016 survey, three in four adults watch YouTube videos on their mobile device. Fast-forward to 2018. Instagram, a mobile-first platform, introduced a new feature: IGTV. The IGTV feature allows its users to upload long-form videos, or videos up to 60 minutes. What do you think of Instagram's new feature? What impact might it have on YouTube? What impact might it have on video sharing?

For More Information

FURTHER READING

Birley, Shane. *How to Be a Blogger and Vlogger in 10 Easy Lessons: Learn How to Create Your Own Blog, Vlog, or Podcast and Get It Out in the Blogosphere!* Lake Forest, CA: Walter Foster Jr., 2016.

Green, Julie. *Shooting Video to Make Learning Fun.* Ann Arbor, MI: Cherry Lake, 2010.

Tashjian, Janet. *My Life as a YouTuber.* New York: Henry Holt and Co., 2018.

Willoughby, Nick. *Digital Filmmaking for Kids for Dummies.* Hoboken, NJ: John Wiley & Sons, Inc., 2015.

Willoughby, Nick. *Making YouTube Videos: Star in Your Own Video!* Hoboken, NJ: John Wiley & Sons, Inc., 2015.

WEBSITES

YouTube—SoulPancake
www.youtube.com/user/soulpancake
Follow SoulPancake for thought-provoking and hilarious videos.

YouTube—EthanGamer
www.youtube.com/user/EthanGamerTV
Journey along with Ethan as he plays *Roblox*, *Minecraft*, and other fun games!

GLOSSARY

auditory (AW-dih-tor-ee) related to hearing

campaigning (kam-PAYN-ing) serving in a series of organized activities in order to achieve a particular goal

censor (SEN-sur) to remove parts of a book, movie, or other work that are thought to be unacceptable or offensive

gameplay (GAYM-play) the way a player interacts with or plays a game

graphic (GRAF-ik) giving a detailed picture of things as they really are

kinesthetic (kin-uhs-THET-ik) learning through feeling

nonprofit (nahn-PRAH-fit) an organization that does business without the purpose of making a profit

podcast (PAHD-kast) an audio file created on the internet for downloading and listening to

retailers (REE-tay-lurz) people who sell goods to customers

viral (VYE-ruhl) message that is spread widely

vloggers (VLAWG-erz) people who post video blogs

web hosting service (WEB HOHST-ing SUR-vis) a service on the internet that allows a person or a business to make a website and publish it online

INDEX